The Pain Cycle

The Pain Cycle

Poems by

Alexandria Wyckoff

© 2024 Alexandria Wyckoff. All rights reserved.
This material may not be reproduced in any form, published,
reprinted, recorded, performed, broadcast,
rewritten or redistributed without
the explicit permission of Alexandria Wyckoff.
All such actions are strictly prohibited by law.

Cover design by Shay Culligan
Cover image by Nathan Dumlao
Author photo by Jamie Lynn Zambri

ISBN: 978-1-63980-499-3

Kelsay Books
502 South 1040 East, A-119
American Fork, Utah 84003
Kelsaybooks.com

*Mom and Dad:
Thank you for always supporting my dream
to become an author.*

*Stephanie:
Thank you for helping me every step of the way.*

Contents

On Turning 17	9
I don't like needles	10
Google Search History of a High School Girl	11
All Chances Lost	13
Dive into My Depths: A Villanelle	14
Alien Goes for a Hike	15
Sealed for Your Protection	17
Thoughts While I Jog for 25 Minutes During PT	19
Snakeskin	22
Poem for the Battle Scars	24
Alien Learns How to Use Elevator Key	26
Gym Class Hero?	27
The Girl with the Injured ACL Writes Her Dream Dictionary	28
The Broken Bird	30
Discarded	31
Google Search History of Alien	32
Recovery™	34
A Pantoum for Summer Break	37
Alien Defines Pain	38
Atonement	40
Yosemite, post knee-surgery	42
The Pain Cycle	43
Alien Encounters an MRI Machine	44
Self-Portrait as Indian Glass Fish	45
Triumph of Me(n)	46
Ignite	47
Alien Becomes Different	49
Winter Light	51
If Frankenstein's Monster Ruptured and Repaired Its ACL	52
Body Barometer	55
A Time Traveler Proves the Pain Cycle	56

On Turning 17

I have two rules on my birthday:

1. be grateful
    when they slice across my knee

2. smile
    when needles pierce my skin and
    flood my veins with drugs

    I try to convince myself: this is exactly what I wanted this
    year.

    Could I go back to the day
    I broke my future?

    Kick the ball away, this fragile
    body, built haphazardly,
    waits for the perfect moment to fall
    apart like a Jenga tower teeters
    back and forth.

    Don't lunge against the hardwood floor;
    that waxy surface, that squeak. My leg takes
    the momentum, collapses onto itself
    with a loud, final snap.

    There was a moment.
    I could have walked away.

I   don't   like   needles

the way they gleam in the light, the sharpened point, the
                                                                                        plunge

that I feel so weak next to something so small, so
                                                                                      fragile

the memories that replay in my skull: a younger me jerks away
                                                                                                  screaming,

the way I still flinch as a doctor injects three nerve-blockers under
                                                                                                       my skin,

that stick in my back between gloved fingertips, numbed body
                                                                                    from the waist down,

the IV probing into my hand to find a vein like invaders search
                                                                                             to destroy.

Google Search History of a High School Girl

After Ocean Vuong

January → what's the best brand of laptop
                                    for college
                                    to get
                                    for gaming
                                    for business
                                    battery

February → suny oswego's honors program basic information

March → section IV softball ranking, gilboa-conesville

April → do you need surgery if you
                                    tear your ACL
                                    tear your meniscus
                                    have gallstones
                                    tear a ligament
                                    have a hernia

Trending: College admissions scandal (Operation Varsity Blues)
Fire at Notre-Dame

May → how long is the recovery process after acl surgery?

June → us women's soccer team world cup standings
Trending: Hong Kong Protests

July → physical therapy locations near me
                      Dr. Megan Mullin Physical Therapy—31.8mi
                      Megamotion Physical Therapy—31.0mi
                      Ostrander Physical Therapy—22.7mi
                      SECO Physical Therapy—18.8mi

August → how can you overextend your ACL graft?
Trending: Toni Morrison dead at 88

September → inspiring senior quotes

"What lies behind us, and what lies before us are small matters compared to what lies within us." ~ Ralph Waldo Emerson

> "Sometimes you will never know the value of a moment until it becomes a memory." ~ Dr. Suess

"You will succeed if you persevere; and you will find a joy in overcoming obstacles." ~ Helen Keller

October → band-aids
- Medline Curad Flex-Fabric Adhesive Bandages, Box of 100 $7.50
- Sterile Flexible Adhesive Bandages, One Size $7.62
- Welly Good Vibes Bravery Badges—Flexible Fabric Bandage—48 count—Assorted Shapes & Styles $7.99

November → how long will my acl graft hurt?

> *Trending: Gun Violence at Home—369 Mass Shootings*

December → *Dirty Dancing* christmas gifts for mom
- Dirty Dancing Framed Memorabilia Legends Never Die $58.99
- I've Had the Time of My Life Dirty Dancing Heart Lyric Music Wall Art Print $13.95
- Dirty Dancing Poster Quilt Blanket Ver 2 $49.99
- Dirty Dancing Gift Kellerman's Candle; I Carried a Watermelon, Nobody Puts Baby in a Corner, I Had the Time of My Life $26.00

Trending: President Donald Trump was impeached; third president in U.S. history

All Chances Lost

No bones / protruded / out of thin skin,
but the fire / sensation / spread

through / my leg.
Doctors issued / a sentence:

six months / of missed opportunities.
The wave of / regrets / engulfed me,

pushed me / to the brink / of sanity,
hands scraping / against rocks / as I collapsed

into myself, / hating / that last goal
in gym class. / I was / stuck / there broken,

waiting / for a scalpel / to fix / what I had
ruptured. / Healing / took months. / I watched

the world go by, / restricted / to crutches
and physical therapy. / My own / two legs

could not / support / the burning in my heart.
No work, / no soccer, / no softball—

instead I / sat on a cliff / of my own / suffering.
Patience / became a skill / learned quickly,

but / never / completely / chased / away
thoughts of disappointment. / They linger

with me / now. / Could I have
explored more / of the craggy mountain

landscapes of Yosemite? / Could I have
embraced / the edge of the world

instead of / cowering / against solid ground?

Dive into My Depths: A Villanelle

I am the still river, brackish and deep;
duckweed and sea grass hide in each soft swerve.
That shimmer in the depths is what you seek,

buried beneath layers of sand that seeps
into the slow current without a word.
I am the still river, brackish and deep.

You found my seashell smile, but when you speak
you struggle to convince me to preserve
this shimmer in the depths of what you seek.

You prize my pebbles piled in small heaps
but these compliments feel so undeserved.
I am the still river, brackish and deep.

My roaming waves shift in the dark, they creep
but your eyes find the shiny white blur and
that shimmer in the depths is what you seek.

Baroque pearls are a prize you want to keep,
but there is danger here, haven't you heard?
There is a still river, brackish and deep,
this shimmer in the depths is what you seek.

Alien Goes for a Hike

The golden light filters through spruce tree tops and through my slanted form. My weight balances on the left foot. Not the right. Metal crutches latch under each arm. Chafed skin, a thick layer I hate to brush these soft fingers over. The adhesives on each scar press against purple and red cuts scraped into my knee, bound together by black wire.

One two three four

of the wounds, a new part of me, stripes across my skin. Will they be here forever? Humans look at me like a specimen with their cruel eyes and sharp tongues.

Click click click click

beneath the green canopy. Rocks block the passage like sentries. Tree stumps like road signs on a long-forgotten path. My knee aches with every

One two three four

step. I stab each crutch into the earth, push and pull my way over scattered bumps, each step planted like a tree sprout. I can't control each limb. I swing forward, destruction in my wake.

Click click click click

My body is unpleasant. In the midday light, glacial run-off sweeps through the valley. Black shorts roll, sneakers off, teeth grit. I plunge my foot into the water. Shock. Right. To. My. Brain.

One two three four

I'm unfit to live here. I belong to a planet with other four-legged Aliens. I watch the water ripple over my feet. It flickers between ten toes and two rubber stumps. Am I human or monster? I raise my head to this foreign world. Here, the sky is brilliant blue. Here, the trees sway. Here, the bugs chirp loudly to each other.

Click   click   click   click

Sealed for Your Protection

I.

This abandoned basement collects dust
in the crevice of my chest:
a table surrounded by bare shelves.
Spiderwebs catch yellow
light from the flickering bulb
suspended from the ceiling.

II.

Her raw fingers set a glass jar
on the surface; bloody smudges
like scarlet rose petals plucked
from their stem. The girl presses
a scalpel to her chest, cuts through
shirt and flesh to reveal an ivory ribcage.
She snaps two ribs like a twig
under a boot and reaches deeper,
slides the organ into the jar with
a bloody gush, pours saline
to the brim, shoves a cork in with a click.
She stores it on a ledge
like a librarian sorts their shelves, and
disappears up the stairs wrapped
around my spinal cord.

III.

The heart is alone; the jar grows
its own sheen of dust—marked passage
of time in a room without a clock.
The heart remains whole, but turns
black after a while and sinks
to the bottom like a broken butterfly;
wings bent and ripped and ruined.

Thoughts While I Jog for 25 Minutes During PT

25
Stretch weary legs, warm from the past thirty minutes of exercise. I step onto the belt, and set the treadmill at a practical speed

24
Maybe this session won't be as bad as yesterday

23
The radio is silent, I only hear the slap of exercise bands, clank of machines, and conversations between doctors and patients

22
I wipe my hands on my shirt, damp streaks darken the cotton fabric

21
Stupid shorts climb my thighs in bunches. I yank them back down

20
Knee is feeling pretty good

19
My feet hitting the treadmill is kind of hypnotic
Thump   Thump   Thump

18
The kid on the stationary bike across the room had knee surgery too, though he needs the support of crutches while I can run around now.
I used to be him.

17
The heat in my body escapes; beads of sweat appear at my hairline and slide down the hollow of my back, collecting at my waistband

16
What homework do I have to do when this is over?

15
I hope everyone is having fun at soccer practice

14
THESE FUCKING SHORTS!

13
I'm halfway through now—I can do this; heartbeat vibrates my chest as it carries oxygen-rich blood to starved muscles

12
I wish for the adrenaline of the soccer field, spectators watching my foot connect with the ball as it flies through the air in a glorious arc; instead, the old man lifting two pound weights gazes at me from across the room

11
I can't believe I have to run this long

10
Calves are tightening up like ropes under immense pressure

9
How many more weeks of PT do I have left?

8
Two people just left the building; the quiet is stifling. Maybe I can sing a song in my head . . .

7
I used to wipe my hands on my shirt before I threw the soccer ball to my teammates. Funny how muscle memory captures a moment in time, bringing me to the past as I unconsciously swipe downwards, again and again

6
Laundry needs to be done when I get home

5
I have to do this two more times this week

4
My doctor checks the time on the treadmill. Her voice melts into the cacophony of sounds
Thump   Thump   Thump

3
DAMN my hamstrings are tight, the ropey tendons refuse to release

2
Just a little further

1
Slow the machine down, slightly limping from the sore ache in my legs.
I'm done

0
I look at the clock on the wall; this took too long
Soccer practice is over.

Snakeskin

You sit on the couch, a black brace

        wrapped around your knee like

                a starving anaconda,

                        maw inches away from your

                    cervix, dripping snake saliva onto

              your bulging thighs. You are a statue

            or you are a threat, so you sit still

          while diamond-shaped pupils track

        miniscule movements, an unhinged jaw slithers up

until your limb disappears

      into the depths of the reptile.

          Every half-hour you slip ice packs

                down the snake's esophagus

                    to cool your skin.

                        Your leg still feels too hot,

                like your flushed face, while

        your heartbeat's in your femur, each

      pulse enhances that frustration,

that inescapable feeling,

          despair rotting in your stomach

                like your leg rots

                      submerged in snake stomach acid.

Poem for the Battle Scars

In the shower,

      soap bubbles wash

over everything.

      The iodine streaks

across my thigh

      like war paint;

I try to scrub it off

      with one hand while

the other grips

      the grab bar. My

knuckles turn white

      from the pressure;

I want to stand on my own,

      not falter and fall

like a broken body hit

      by a wayward bullet.

After my legs failed,

        I became allies with the bar,

battled the slippery

        fiberglass while

the pain in my leg seared;

        damage from a war

I never wanted.

        Bitterness

lodged in my knee

        like a piece of shrapnel

I can never pull out.

Alien Learns How to Use Elevator Key

I rub my finger against the golden teeth
until the key warms to my touch.
This silver spaceship will transport me
to all of my classes. It hovers at the basement floor.
Automated doors hiss open, sulfurous smoke
pours and billows into the hallway and over my metal limbs.

But there is no smoke, just the flickering light
in the ceiling, and the musty smell of an unused elevator
like petrichor wafts through the air in spring.
The cabin shakes under my lifeless legs.
A white glow draws my eye like a firework exploding
in the night. I push *one*. Doors close with a shuddering sigh;

the spaceship jolts upward and I brace
for impact, a quivering heap of alloy and flesh.
The doors yawn open. Nobody sees my form flee,
my shadow stumbles across the cobalt blue lockers.
I thump rhythmically to my next class, this internal clock
accelerates with each   *click*   *click*   *click*

like a bomb about to detonate.

Gym Class Hero?

My opponents glare across the line
so I serve them a haughty smile
on a silver platter. Nothing can beat
this moment; yellow ball drops dead center,
players adjust their pinnies, the sharp trill of the whistle
as the game erupts like Mauna Loa.

I kick the ball across the line, my teammate
punches it into the right side of the net. The whistle
blows and we cheer through the tying goal.
One more point floats in my vision like a mirage;
I scramble toward the ball and sweat

pools at the base of my back. I suck
filtered air into my lungs. My team whacks my body
with high-fives and slaps on the shoulder while we wait
for the game to begin again. I am balanced on a ladder
of confidence.

The ball at my feet again as I surge up the side of the field
like an electric current toward the opponent.
Right leg shoots outward

I   go   down.

My leg collapses like a stack of cards;
the pain is everywhere and nowhere,
the scorching sensation radiates up and down.

Was it worth it?

                            Was   it?

The Girl with the Injured ACL Writes Her Dream Dictionary

After Nick Carbó

Flying: Avoidance, cowardice, shame.
1. Flying solo—Keep your feelings to yourself.
2. Flying blind—Take baby steps; your left leg bears the weight of your tired body.

Yellow: Stay far away from this color. It's evil.

Chairs: You need support.
          See—Family, Friends.

Aliens: A reflection of yourself. A void that swallows the light as frigid air burns exposed skin. Stars blink in the distance while you drift near a black hole.

Surgeon: Modern-day superhero.
        Synonyms—Doctor, Physician, Bearer of bad news.
        Antonyms—Wizard or witch (magic healers), Friend.

Stairs: Avoid at all costs.
        Stare, verb: Everyone runs past you. Look forward, not back.

Purple: You're projecting. Not everything is bruised.

Satellite: You will not find the answers you're searching for.

Fist-bump: Travel to grassy fields where your friends play soccer. Support them. Maybe they will return the favor.

Spiderwebs: You'll figure everything out.
    1. Spiders—Bad omens.
        1. See—Doctor, Gym, Soccer, Teammates.
    2. Housefly—Your hopes and dreams.
        1. See—Future, Soccer, Healing, Goals.

Windows: Find a hammer. Collect the shards. This is how far you've come.

Broken glass: This is your heart.

The Broken Bird

Seven daring ducklings
in a perfect little row with
feathers brown as tree bark.

Three small bodies are covered
in velvety down and they peer through
slitted eyes, practically just-born.

Others have grown first feathers, flap
wings over and over but their
feet never leave the ground.

Two more have their wings outstretched
to the heavens before they leap off the cliff, soar
like the sun is a homing beacon.

The last duck has flown the longest,
but her feathers got singed by the sun.
One wing stable while the other hangs
crooked, bone splintered and bruised.

Discarded

The whistle blows / I'm on the other side of the field / playing Assistant Coach / (more like Team Reject) / stranded / on a bench while teammates / run / down an expanse of green / My foot taps / like a stopwatch / the ball so close / (the opposing team just scored) / At the end of the first half / sweaty bodies huddle / I hover / outside / answer questions / hold in criticism / (their passes like four-year-old bumblebee soccer) / (they stick to the ball like golden honey) / I give a thumbs up to Coach / who paces / back and forth / until she groans, rests her head in her hands / (I would have made that last goal) / (I would have kept us in the game) / They take advantage of their / healthy / bodies / Mine looks fine / (My knee joints click, bones slide like overworked clock gears) / but I stand / trapped / in a body I don't want / while the play clock hits zero / the horn echoes across the field /

Google Search History of Alien

After Ocean Vuong

what are the benefits of four
> **wheel drive**
> **day work week**
> **years of college**
> **legs**

how to use an elevator
- *How to Ride an Elevator: 15 steps (with Pictures)* — WikiHow
- *Elevator use for dummies* —Elevator Wiki—Fandom
- *Don't Push the Wrong Buttons: Learn Good Elevator Etiquette* —Nationwide Lifts
- *Elevators or stairs?* —National Institute of Health (.gov)

what is an mri machine
> → *National Institute of Health (NIH)* "Magnetic Resonance Imaging (MRI) is a non-invasive image technology that produces three dimensional detailed anatomical images"

> why is an mri machine loud
>> → *The New York Times* "The banging is the vibration of metal coils in the machine caused by rapid pulses of electricity"

>> why can't you have metal in an mri machine
>>> → *ARA Diagnostic Imaging* "Since MRI uses a very strong magnet, metal on or inside the body may be affected, so be sure to tell your scheduler and technologist about any device . . ."

popular hikes in yosemite
- Vernal and Nevada Falls Trail → Elevation 2,000 feet; two breathtaking waterfalls
- North Dome Trail → Elevation 8,100 feet; spectacular views across Tenaya Canyon
- Lower Yosemite Falls Hike → Elevation 4,000 feet; tallest waterfall in North America, 5th in the world
- Dewey Point Trail → Elevation 7,316 feet; sweeping panorama of Yosemite Valley

what is antarctica

Dec 8, 2010 (NASA.gov) **Antarctica is a continent.** It is Earth's fifth largest continent. Antarctica is covered in ice. Antarctica covers Earth's South Pole.

Wikipedia.com **Antarctica is . . . [the] least-populated continent.**

What type of heart is human?
→ "The human heart is a four-chambered muscular organ, shaped and sized roughly like a man's closed fist with two-thirds of the mass to the left of midline. The heart is enclosed in a pericardial sac that is lined with the parietal layers of a serous membrane."

People also ask:
Is the heart skeletal?
What is the heart of a person?

Recovery™

Welcome to physical therapy.

L e v e l O n e

You will need to stand on your own.

The forest ahead is full of gnarled roots
and vines; a green sea ripples in the sunlight.

> Initial skills: quad muscle constrictions
> Boss: walk without crutches

L e v e l T w o

Congratulations, you are walking.

You stumble against an exposed tree root.
The light dims. Birds call overhead, their voices
whisper in your mind.

> Initial skills: stationary bike
> Boss: leg extension 0°

L e v e l T h r e e

You think you're doing well?

Those voices in your head grow louder, then deeper.
Shadows reach to grasp the newly healed flesh
of your leg. You grab a stick and swat them away,
like a swarm of flies that buzz over a carcass.

> Initial skills: exercise ball balance
> Boss: 3lb hamstring lifts

Level Four

You will sweat from now until the end.

The trees are thick, the temperature rises as you pass
the epicenter. Salty droplets fall into your eyes
and slither down your back. A growl echoes across
the wilderness—you pause.

> Initial skills: ladder drills
> Boss: 2 ½ lb leg lifts

Level Five

You're strong, but clunky.

The beast crashes through the bushes, pounces.
Branches and leaves snap against your skin
as you stare into the eyes of a wolf—yellow like
the iodine lathered across your thigh before surgery.
You push against the muscular form, hard
like the stones that grind into your cheek.

> Initial skills: lunges
> Boss: jog for 15 minutes

Level Six

You will not win.

The wolf opens its jaws, exposes white canines desperate
to slice into your neck. You grab a rock and smash

it into the animal; it collapses on top of you. The weight
settles onto your chest—you are trapped, no way out.

Initial skills: skipping
Boss: one-legged jump test

This Game Never Ends

A Pantoum for Summer Break

Have a great summer!
My classmates cheered as they raced
out the door toward the yellow streak of buses
while I wobbled with crutches.

As my classmates raced away,
excited about their last soccer camp together
I wobbled with crutches,
frustrated with my broken body.

Their last soccer camp without me
filled my sleepless nights;
frustrated with my broken body
that would take six months to heal.

A summer of sleepless nights
stretched out in front of me; an ACL injury
would take six months to heal.
Have a great summer.

Alien Defines Pain

Wet concrete grit digs
into the pads of my rubber

               feet. It adds to the
               click   click   click

sound of metal joints and the soft
taps of raindrops

               on my upturned face. Cold
               drizzle dampens the heat

of a late June night. I inch
closer to the building (school).

               The door looms ahead, its glass
               windows protects all of the visitors

(it lingers on me). I pass through,
step onto tile with soaked rubber

               feet, and slide like a penguin[1] down
               an icy slope. My flesh limb

catches me, but
my heart[2] drops

               onto the floor,
               slaps the white tiles.

Will this blinding light
tear through my body again[3],

---

[1] Aquatic flightless bird that live almost exclusively in the Southern Hemisphere
[2] Fist-sized organ that pumps blood throughout your body

                my damaged[4] knee always
                a target for disaster. I shuffle

forward, peel[5] my heart
off the floor and drop it into

                my pocket. All four legs stumble
                to the parking lot. My heart

only beats again when I'm
in my car and no one can see

                tears stream down my face,
                or the (slight) shake[6] of my hands as they

grip the steering wheel.

---

[3] Synonyms: petrified, horrified, frightened
[4] Antonyms: healthy, perfect, unbroken
[5] To strip off an outer layer of; to come off in sheets or scales
[6] Antonyms: soothe, reassure, strengthen

Atonement

According to research, an ACL tear is one acute injury that female athletes are two to eight times more likely to experience than males.
—Carrie Macmillan (Yale Medicine/2020)

The male physique—
that steadfast fortitude,
that unhindered strength.

Bones assembled like a cathedral, tendons
strapped to muscles as they flex.
Modern mosaic full of complex texture;

a vessel made for something
more than childbirth.
Fat laced through my muscles

like prime rib, marbled in shades of
white and red. Breasts scattered with
yellow globs of fatty tissue, puckered

by lines of cellulite.
A body created from a lone rib
will never work as well,

this careless construction
won't perform. I crumbled like a sandcastle
beneath the waves of

the masculine model.
From above, the moon watched
and wept blue light. I waded into

the salty ocean, dipped my broad hips
in, hoped that water would cleanse
this body. I emerged from the liquid

onto coarse sand, salt crusted over my
skin like the tattoos of my sins.
I screamed my repentance into the air

to the world that prizes the Adam over the Eve.

Yosemite, post knee-surgery

The breeze brushes across my
face; a concerned mother's caress.

Mountains, soldiers protecting
the land, glance back at me.

The sun glints off the metal
handrails—a constant reminder

of human interference. I shift,
try to emulate the broad shoulders,

sharp jawlines of those stoic
warriors, but I cannot raise

my chest high enough.
For how can one be a fighter

trapped by crutches under each
arm; chafed skin revealing my

soft exterior? I relent, instead gaze
towards deep trenches hidden

among each rank, where
battles continue to rage on—

faint roadways cutting into trees
like scratches on well-worn armour.

Footprints slowly spread like a disease.

The Pain Cycle

Snowflakes float to the ground outside the glass
while I sit with knee propped, lathered in cream.
White blanket smothers the last green grass,
this ache seeps from my scar between the seams.

I stare out at nothing and everything,
distract my mind from a pain that lingers
and drags up my knee, unlike anything
I've ever felt. I push down with fingers

frozen from the cold; even the fire
can't chase away this winter, or the ice
crystalized through muscle like steel wire.
I feel like I'm trapped in a weather vise.

The sun peeks through and the pain fades away,
but there will always be more snowy days.

Alien Encounters an MRI Machine

Waiting rooms make my heart jump
and others sneak glances
at my four legs, whisper to their
neighbors until my name is called.

I hunch in like a hedgehog as I
click   click   click
to a private room where the man
watches me, his face a mask
built from countless hours
caring for the broken and weak.

"No metal in this room."

His voice rolls over me
like velvet. My metal limbs detach
from the crevices
underneath my arms. He
leads me in; he smells like cinnamon but then

the machine glowers at me,
sleek and sinister. Its mouth gapes open,
teeth glint in the light while its tongue protrudes.
The man straps me onto the table, leg locked in
a lattice of straps and ties.
Before he escapes, he plugs my ears.

The monster groans to life and sucks me
into its depths, I open my mouth when
click   click   click
surrounds me like a heartbeat. Recognition,
like the dents scattered across my metal legs
made of memories beyond the stars,

it calls my name.

Self-Portrait as Indian Glass Fish

After Aimee Nezhukumatathil

I cower, your needle hovers
        above the surface—peeks
                through water sprites with a silver wink.

I swim alone in the tank—
        you stole the others and made
                a rainbow of their bodies.

My heart trembles through the window of my scales
        behind miniscule rib bones.
                Flimsy protection, like a rusted cage.

Your fingers dip into the water, pinch my tail—
        the needle splits apart my exterior
                as bubbles escape my mouth.

Dye floods through; this fuchsia death,
        the foreign weight of color
                leaches into my bloodstream.

Triumph of Me(n)

When my hamstring was a brittle band (cracked dry rot, the color of dirt) I found a Bible (hidden) in the basement. I searched its pages; I stretched the limits. Who wouldn't? When anacondas slide their prey down acidic gullets, skin pulls taut around meat. The hinge will open. When shellfish endure torrents of waves, they crash into sand, two sides (of a whole) clamped shut. Prove them (all) wrong, find a way to return (no matter how hard). This mismatched body is more than a lone (spare / used) rib.

Ignite

Rip out those tendrils of
         core ligament that
         snap in the harsh wind like

Electrical wires.

Cut the hamstring short
         like a sentence caught
         in your throat; you

Only need nine inches. Your body

Never used cadaver parts extracted
         from a chest full of
         ice, hearts, and lungs until now.

Sometimes you have to get
         a little dead inside.

To reattach a new ACL, you must

Relinquish the control of your body,
         become anesthetized

Under the knives of doctors
         and keyhole incisions.
         The blades creep

Closer to the live wires buzzing
         inside surrounded
         by pliable muscle.

Tomorrow you'll be home, knee propped
                                      up as you sink into
                                      the soft couch but

Instead of this dead space,
                you will have a current
                that surges

Over fuses braided and braced;
                          these four

New scars spark.

Alien Becomes Different

I begin in a cold room with harsh
lights that glare into an empty
chest cavity, highlight the paths

of tears over sunken cheeks.
A woman asks my height
(why should it matter?) and

returns with my new legs.
Monotone gray and cold, like the room,
like Antarctica. She approaches

my body with the limbs, pokes her fingers
beneath each armpit to locate
my ports. Each device snaps into place

like it was always meant to be there.
(Am I supposed to be this way?)
The metal warms to my touch,

I brace my palms against handles
and push up, watch rubber fold
over as it keeps my body

off the ground. I wait for the crack
against the pressure, but the tips hold,
resolute. Not even an earthquake

could cause me to tumble.
Click   click   click
echoes in the small room as I move

faster, like a grizzly bear prowls through
the underbrush, a predator stalking its prey.
(Everyone should have four legs.)

The woman bares teeth
and retreats to the farthest
corner in the room.

Winter Light

Lyrics taken from The Weeknd's song "Blinding Lights"

I'm drowning in the night

The lake around my bed rises as tears drip down full of regret and hate. My body is poisonous. Tear ducts open and close like floodgates; irises bob in the water, eyelashes drip as liquid spills over the brim. My cheeks burn, red streaks follow the path of my sorrow. The toxins replenish as I sleep.

Ohh, I'm blinded by the lights

across my vision as I am transferred to the operating room. The metal is cold against my back where the gown ties together, the chill seeps through the white sheets. A figure blocks the brightness overhead. A mask puts me to sleep.

I'm just calling back to let you know

Six months has made me patient. The phone rings as the sun descends; the doctor doesn't need to see me again. Progress is a wonderful thing. I cross the Threshold of Recovery toward the Land of Being Healed. My dreams turn peaceful as I sleep.

The city's cold and empty / No one's around to judge me

The snow crunches underneath two boots. The mail waits for me at the end of the driveway. Cold earbuds blast music, the barren trees creak in the wind as I spin and laugh into the dusk.

If Frankenstein's Monster Ruptured and Repaired Its ACL

the ends

of my smile

are fixed

with screws

but this torn

ligament, this issue

in the middle

of my leg

nestled between

tibia and femur

feels like a cello

string stretched

to its limits.

unlike the

mangled muscle

carelessly smashed

by hacksaws

and staples,

probes and scalpels

healed me this

time. minimally

invasive

procedures make

this life so

convenient.

specimens harvested

from cadaver

and hamstring,

folded and coiled

into a segment

ready for weight.

my lurching

walk is a thing

of the past,

stiff joints

don't burden

me now. steps

fall faster and

faster as i run

into the wind,

wrenching my

smile to its limits.

i pull fresh air into

my mismatched lungs

while villagers

point and scream

like i am

some kind

of monster.

Body Barometer

Rain slaps the windshield in a calm
monotony but all I feel is the hollow

pulse in my knee; a heartbeat that circulates
throbbing blood and bruises inside of my body.

My fingers push into scar tissue but I can't
reach the inner rot in the joint. The smell floats

inside the car, burns my nostrils like garbage
that has baked in the sun for hours. Maggots feast;

their milky white bodies slither across cartilage
to munch on sweet bone marrow. I wonder

if the doctors left a blade inside when they pulled
me apart and crammed me back together—

I feel it burrow through muscle and tissue like a mole
trying to find warmth in the frigid earth.

A Time Traveler Proves the Pain Cycle

Inspired by Fabio Valerio Sciarretta's "History of anterior cruciate ligament surgery."

I: July, 1839

Balmy dew sticks to my skirts
while I fly through the grassy fields
like a barn swallow.
Night knocks at the door of my vision,

shadows peer behind trees.
Joseph shouts and stumbles over
brambles and rocks, his delicate leather shoes
scratched and fraying at the seams.

The crest of the hill rises like the morning sun
while the real star sinks below the horizon.
I watch yellow burn with Joseph,
his broad chest rises and falls like the waves

of the Atlantic. I dare him with a glance
and down the hill we go, screeches filter
into the quiet summer air.
Legs jerk and slip as I hit a hole

in the ground, a snap and I collapse.
The boy reaches the bottom of the hill
with a war cry, my skirts
anchor around my wounded body.

My right knee loose, bones scrape
and I feel like a rag doll. Sturdy arms
carry me home to Dr. James Stark, to
a dingy room, to a leg examined

under candlelight. Scarlet blood drips
on braces strapped around like metal cuffs.
My home a prison; friends turn away,
drapes are pulled, and candles burn out.

After two weeks of wrapping braces
too tight against bruising flesh, I fling
the windows open and escape the land
where I broke my first body.

II: October, 1934

Mary's knee is the size
of a watermelon, full
of fluid after her leg twisted
on the wooden dance floor.

Our dance partners rush her away
into the brisk night air, stars wink as
my eyebrows close like curtains.
I climb in next to her prone form.

The hospital is small and smells
like death as coughs and cries
fill the air. I pace by her bed,
knee aching with sympathy—

a reminder of my last life.
Dr. Galeazzi conducts the orchestra
of Mary's body; plucks the new
hamstring graft as it nestles under

three incisions. Her leg is wrapped
like a cocoon, one stiff brace keeps
her straight, tucked beneath layers of
crisp white sheets and cords.

Tentative steps with crutches
transform into small exercises until
Mary's body grows strong. Incisions fade.
Her brace falls away.

I smile, a false face,
while jealousy rages in the spaces
between my ribs. It tries to claw
at Mary but I wrap my arms tight

as the pressure increases with each breath.
Mary shoots through the green pasture,
her laughter drifts over hills as she runs faster
than I ever could. The year my friend

stretched her ligament too far. The year
that feels like 100 years shoved into
the crevices in my right knee. I fade
away into the ebb and flow of time.

III: April, 2019

The ball taps my foot
as I dribble and shoot, the floor wax
reflects the glint of my teeth. A sharp
trill of the whistle restarts the game.

I steal the ball with
a honed kick. My opponent attacks
and I try to defend, but my hallowed knee
cracks and digs like a shovel

pushing through old dirt on
an unmarked grave. Time travelers
have little say about this kind of resurrection.
Doctor's offices reek of antiseptics

and foreshadowing as fierce
as a ten blade. I never meet the doctor;
this is like wrapping a band-aid
on a paper cut. Nerves needle

my mind as I fall into the anesthesia.
Braces and crutches carry me until
they shed away like a second skin,
limbs reawaken from the hamstring

and cadaver ligament graft. But this time
there is finally a break in the cycle: revival.
I chase the sun as it dips
below the horizon.

About the Author

Alexandria Wyckoff has previously been published in *The Ana, Quillkeepers Press, The Pensieve, Planisphere Q,* and others. From a small town called Gilboa in New York, Alexandria received her BA in Creative Writing from SUNY Oswego. She is currently working in the publishing industry writing and editing articles. This is her first collection of poetry.

www.ingramcontent.com/pod-product-compliance
Lightning Source LLC
Chambersburg PA
CBHW031205160426
43193CB00008B/517